Nottinghamshire
Edited by Claire Tupholme

 Young**Writers**

First published in Great Britain in 2007 by:
Young Writers
Remus House
Coltsfoot Drive
Peterborough
PE2 9JX
Telephone: 01733 890066
Website: www.youngwriters.co.uk

SB ISBN 978-1 84602 935 6

Foreword

Young Writers was established in 1991 and has been passionately devoted to the promotion of reading and writing in children and young adults ever since. The quest continues today. Young Writers remains as committed to the nurturing of poetic and literary talent as ever.

This year's Young Writers competition has proven as vibrant and dynamic as ever and we are delighted to present a showcase of the best poetry from across the UK and in some cases overseas. Each poem has been selected from a wealth of *Little Laureates* entries before ultimately being published in this, our sixteenth primary school poetry series.

Once again, we have been supremely impressed by the overall quality of the entries we have received. The imagination, energy and creativity which has gone into each young writer's entry made choosing the poems a challenging and often difficult but ultimately hugely rewarding task - the general high standard of the work submitted ensured this opportunity to bring their poetry to a larger appreciative audience.

We sincerely hope you are pleased with this final collection and that you will enjoy *Little Laureates Nottinghamshire* for many years to come.

Contents

Lewis Bryce Humphreys (9)   69
Megan Unwin (11)   70
Chloe Allen (8)   71
Brody Asher (9)   72
Callum Boorman (8)   73
Joanne Heathcote (8)   74
Alex Michael Chadwick (8)   75
Edward Turner (9)   76
Siân Hudson (10)   77
Phoebe-Lois Brown (10)   78
Katy Bramley (9)   79
Hazel Surgey (7)   80
Hannah Elson (7)   81
Hollie Bidwell (7)   82
Natalie Walpole (8)   83
Abigail Louise Wright (9)   84
Jessica Southall (10)   85
Eleanor Boultby (10)   86
Cara Williams (10)   87
Bradley Perkins (8)   88
Hayley Goodwin (9)   89
Leanne Creasey (11)   90
Daniel Wright (9)   91
Katrina Ellingworth (8)   92
Sarah Titterton (8)   93
Hannah Collis (10)   94
Eleanor Gladman (8)   95
Elise Diamond Radford (8)   96
Eleanor Bunting (8)   97
Ethan Thrower (9)   98

Redlands Primary School
Georgia Barrowcliffe (10)   99
Lauren Morris (10)   100
Jake Milson & Jordanna Williams (10)   101
Emma Tuke (10) & Bethany Roberts (11)   102
Ainsley Kirk (11)   103
Victoria Johnson & Lewis Linacre (10)   104
Nathan Chambers (11)   105
Bayley Pimperton-Vergeldt & Jessie Gilham (10)   106
Nathan Singleton (11)   107

Ashlie Kelly & Chloe Pressley (11)	108
Laura Harwin (11) & Danielle Dickinson (10)	109
Megan Berridge & Elinor Brophy (11)	110
Lawrence Mitchell (11) & Ross Prince (10)	111
Alicia Kirkland (11)	112
Gabrielle Lee (10) & Chloe Schofield (11)	113
Alex Cooke & Connah-Marie Locke (10)	114
Laura Reed (10) & Ashley Lacey (11)	115
Nathan Owen & Oliver Pingree (10)	116
Jade Duckmanton (10)	117
Jamie Park (10)	118
Sheridan Proctor (11)	119
Connah-Marie Locke (10)	120

St Margaret Clitherow RC Primary School, Bestwood Park

Keri-Anne Harrison (9)	121
Clara Dunphy (10)	122
Rosie Blyton Flewitt (9)	123
Callum Asher (10)	124
Sinead Shaw (9)	125
Curtis Kilcullen (9)	126
Jack Northridge (9)	127
Bamu Fru (10)	128
Jessica Carney (9)	129
Caitlin Wall (8)	130
Connor Hopkins (9)	131
Holly Chapman (10)	132
Jareth Evens (10)	133
Enya Powell (10)	134
Kyra Foster (11)	135
Rianna Skeete (11)	136
Rosie Burke (10)	137
Bill Dallman (10)	138
Andre Skeete (7)	139
Ama Fru (8)	140
Shola Thomas-Lewis (7)	141
Lucy Smith (8)	142
Taylor Wright (7)	143
Shannon Gaskell-Henson (8)	144
Sam Chapman (7)	145

The Poems

Pets

Some pets like to bark
And some like to play
Some pets like to purr
And some have messy fur
Some pets are slow
Some pets are low
Some pets bounce
And some like to pounce.

Demi Hogan (7)
Broomhill Junior School

Magic Pot!

My pot is magic!
Real-life magic!

In go wiggly worms
That squiggle and squirm
Next goes slimy slugs
And other delicious bugs!

Mix it, stir it
Round and round
Quiet, silent
Not a sound!

In goes a toad
That I saw down the road.

Mix it, stir it
Round and round
Quiet, silent
Not a sound!

I am a witch
Magic, with my magic pot
Do you believe me
Or dare you not?

I will eat my stew
Yum! Yum! Yum!
Just to fill my tum-tum - tum!
When I have done
I will do a big *burp!*
I am a witch!
Remember I have no manners
Let's have a party
With a big banner
Saying . . .

Witches galore!

Let's do more!

The party's on
We've all had our stew
Let's settle down and
Let's have a snooze!

Lucy Kennedy (10)
Broomhill Junior School

Holidays

Shimmering summer sun,
Clear summer sky,
Aeroplanes flying high.
Lovely beaches,
Lovely sea,
Crowds of people singing in key.

Shimmering summer sun,
Clear summer sky,
Aeroplanes flying high.
Donkey rides,
Cold ice creams,
These are the things of my dreams.

Haylie Hewitt (11)
Broomhill Junior School

Holiday

H appy times to remember
O n all the fantastic rides
L oads of delicious candy and yummy sweets
I t's the most fantastic time of the year
D oing everything that's fun and fantastic
A nd all the time, you're laughing
Y ou really won't forget it!

Craig Thomas (10)
Broomhill Junior School

Friends

Friends are very important
Wherever you go
They are always there for you
Whatever you do
You don't have to worry
They will play with you
They will be there
The whole way through
They're
Trustworthy
Reliable
Helpful
Kind
Nice and
Caring
My best friends.

Kestra Peutrill (10)
Broomhill Junior School

Weather

The sun reminds me of a smile in summer
The moon is like a silver coin glistening on the ground
The clouds are sheep floating nearby
The stars are jewels fallen from the Queen's crown
Raindrops are teardrops falling from a sad face
Thunder is like giant footsteps across the sky
Lightning is like the speed of a racing car.

John Scrimshaw (11)
Broomhill Junior School

My Idol

I have black hair like night-time shades
I am as secret as a midnight raid ·
My eyes are as blue as a laser light
The future of my life is bright
I see me as champ
My muscles aren't weak
I am as strong as a wooden clamp
I never back down
I never quit
I am John Cena.

Christopher Sidebotham (11)
Broomhill Junior School

Summer

Stunning summer sun,
Shining lovely all day,
Hot as fire,
As sharp as glass,
So powerful,
So painful,
As long as a laser,
As bright as the world,
Always a delight,
Twinkling and sparkling,
It's summer sunshine.

Katie Brownlow (11)
Broomhill Junior School

Life Is Just!

Life is just a mess
But I couldn't care less,
Let's put it to the test
Before I guess.

Life is just cool
I don't want to go to school,
I feel like jumping in a pool
But I don't rule.

Life is just a muddle
Let's go play a puzzle,
I want a cuddle
And to jump in a puddle.

Katie Waldron (11)
Cantrell Primary School

At Home, At Home

At home, at home
My sister is always on the phone.

At school, at school
People say that Year 6 rule.

At the park, at the park
No one goes there after dark.

In the car, in the car
Me and my dad go really far.

In space, in space
There is an alien that's a mental case.

On my street, on my street
There are people that I like to greet.

Rochelle Daniel (11)
Cantrell Primary School

Our Teacher

Mrs Weaver's our teacher
She acts so cool
And she knows she's not a fool
But she wants us to have a pool

Mrs Potts is our teacher
She so hates peanuts
And she's not at all nuts

Our head teacher Mrs Cranstone
She doesn't like us throwing stones
Or pushing, kicking, punching and more.

Ulera Longwe (10)
Cantrell Primary School

School

School is not cool,
The teachers think they rule
We're always doing tests,
Never get a rest
We play about all the time
And then the clock strikes nine
It is now time for assembly,
But I have to sit next to Wendy.

Shannon Stapley (11)
Cantrell Primary School

People In My Life

I have a lot of friends
Who are friendly

I have two brothers
Who are good to me

I have some cousins
Who are friends with me

I have a mum and dad
Who provide me with money!

Matthew Gawronski (11)
Cantrell Primary School

School

We go swimming
And we are thinking
We are always winning.

We get told off
Basically a lot
But we do stop.

Beating down
Under the sun
We have
Very much fun.

We go on trips
And the teacher
Is always
Giving us tips!

Alex Galloway (11)
Cantrell Primary School

Friends

My friends are special
And cool
I see them every day
Some act like fools
But kind in every way.

Lauren Deakin (10)
Cantrell Primary School

My Spider-Man Poem

Spider-Man, Spider-Man
Is so great
But when it's down to villains
He's late.

He fights the Green Goblin
And he succeeds
And round New York
He does good deeds.

He swings round town
Pulling buildings down.

Spider-Man's web
Spins like mad
And soon he might just
Become a dad!

In Spider-Man II
He loses his powers
But gives Mary Jane
Some flowers.

Ross Guy (11)
Cantrell Primary School

My Xbox 360

My 360 is my best friend ever,
Play on it too much and you won't become clever.
'Saints Row', 'Just Cause', 'Smackdown vs Raw',
If you start a season, prepare for a war.
So why don't you come to mine to play,
On this stupid and miserable day.

Kieran Bingham (11)
Cantrell Primary School

School

School is sometimes good
School is sometimes bad
Sometimes it's alright
Sometimes it makes you sad

School is alright
It makes you laugh
School dinners
Are just like going to the café

School is fun
When it's PE
We do lots of activities.

Tara Searcey (11)
Cantrell Primary School

Baking Cakes

Bake, mix, make, press,
Try not to spill it on your dress.
If you do, you'll make a mess
And if you do, you won't be happy.
Mum will scream, Dad will shout,
Baby isn't happy, 'Oh no, I'm out!'
I think you can see why baby isn't happy,
Because someone spilt the chocolate on his nappy!
The kitchen is clean, the oven is hot,
The cake is beautiful and we like it a lot!
So if you understand what's going on,
You must think that we're number one!

That's the end of my poem,
I am sad to say,
But let's save the rest
For another day!

Sophie Whyman (8)
Cantrell Primary School

Magical Birds

Cheerily chirping in the early day
Soaring over the water's bay

Birds singing all day long
Sitting on Big Ben, *ding-dong*

Standing in the trees
Feeling the breeze

Birds flying overhead
Some people fill with dirty dread

I don't know why
They start to cry

I think it's when . . .
They've got a white blob on their head!

Daniel Faulconbridge (11)
Cantrell Primary School

Football

Monday
I mastered my inside kick,
But all my teammates took the mick.

Tuesday
I learned how to be a goalkeeper,
Though my feet kept sinking deeper.

Wednesday
I kept on hitting the post,
But that night I saw a ghost.

Thursday
I did a throw-in,
But then I had to go straight for the gin.

Friday
I dashed really fast,
Around the telegraph mast.

Saturday
The manager gave us positions,
But gave me a special mission.

Sunday
Finally the day of the match
And I got through it without a scratch.

Steven Lawton (10)
Cantrell Primary School

Rules Of The Playground

If it's your first day at school
This poem will make you drool.
As you step on the playground
I will tell you why to stay around.
Even though it looks big and scary
And the teachers are very hairy.
When you know the rules of the playground
You'll be fine in time.
Here they are, the rules of the playground
Now I know you'll definitely stay around.

Don't snitch on people older than you!
Act like you know everything!
Join in every game even if it's always the same.
Always acts the innocent one.
Now there is only one more to go
Don't hang around with nerdy kids
They'll teach you how to make fire with twigs.

George Cokkinos (11)
Cantrell Primary School

Diary Poem

Monday
First day back at school
Shivering like a bear
Scared of what might happen.

Tuesday
I'm always in a hurry
But still stop for my McFlurry
Then my fries and drink too.

Wednesday
I got stopped by the headmistress
For running in the corridor
But I stopped straight away.

Thursday
I was in detention
Just because I got a suspension
For not paying for my detention.

Friday
The end of school
But I had an excellent day
I got to play all day.

Charlotte Lipson-Foster (11)
Cantrell Primary School

Me And My Sister

Me and my sister make a great team
We always know how to make my brother go up in steam
On Monday we chucked him in the river
We made him shake and shiver
On Tuesday we tortured him
Then put him in the bin
Wednesday was his day off
Until we gave him some exploding toff
Thursday he did my hair
I ended up looking a scare
On Friday it was a commotion
We sprayed each other with lotion
Saturday, Sunday the same as Monday
Then we start again.

Molly Price (11)
Cantrell Primary School

The Snowy Street

Monday
The snow glistening like crystals in the light,
Footprints appearing when people walk.

Tuesday
Icicles falling off the trees,
Breaking when they fall.

Wednesday
Dogs frozen standing still,
Cats trying to move.

Thursday
People are wearing warm clothes,
When children are having a doze.

Friday
Children crying that the snow has gone,
When adults are singing a song.

Teegan Smith (10)
Cantrell Primary School

School!

If only school was cool
And it had a swimming pool,
Then I would want to come to school.

If only school was cool
And we could play snooker and pool
And no one called people fools.

If only school was cool
And you didn't eat gruel,
We would think school is cool.

Amy Sturman (10)
Cantrell Primary School

My Diary Poem About School

Monday
I am always in a hurry
But I still stop off for my McFlurry.

Tuesday
I went to class
But I fell on a piece of glass.

Wednesday
I went to play
When it was a sunny day.

Thursday
I went for my lunch
But I got hit with a big punch.

Friday
I was having a good day
I wish I could stay.

Cameron Kimbley (11)
Cantrell Primary School

Luck

Monday
I had a bad day
Even though it was a fine day in May.

Tuesday
Wasn't any better
Until I got the winning letter

Wednesday
My luck had turned around
And you'll never guess what I found!

Thursday
Yesterday I found a twenty pound note, cool
But I spent it all on sweets, what a fool!

Friday
I lost all of my luck
And fell in a pile of muck, *yuck!*

Charlotte Smith   (11)
Cantrell Primary School

My Cousin

My cousin is so great,
He once slipped on some slate,
He had to go to hospital for stitches to his head,
Then he went straight home to bed,
To rest his little head,
Oh, poor, poor, poor Ed.

Then he woke up as jolly as joy,
But to realise his stitches,
Had turned to witches,
Right outside his door,
His head hurt even more,
Oh, poor, poor, poor Ed!

Laura Bannister (10)
Cantrell Primary School

The Weekend

The weekend is the best time of the week
Saturday I got lost in the woods, playing hide-and-seek.

Got bullied by my little sister
Least I'm not the one with a blister!

Sunday night the worst night ever
Hurrying and scurrying to do my homework
The week has just started again!

Whitney Kneen (11)
Cantrell Primary School

My Hazardous House

In my house, my white sofa is black
And my cream sink is filled with tooth plaque
My dirty living room walls are painted plain
But on them there's just the odd coffee stain
Our TV has gone up to TV heaven
It only happened when I was seven
My breathless toilet stinks
That's why our noses shrink
But I know one thing for sure
We are not breaking the law.

Aimee Elizabeth Lindley (9)
Cantrell Primary School

My Family

My mother's like a butterfly,
So beautiful and light,
So delicate and colourful,
She sure is very bright.

My father's like a caterpillar,
So peculiar and small,
So fragile and so peaceful,
With a lot of legs to crawl.

My nana's like a ladybird,
So pretty and so kind,
So cute and detailed perfectly,
But so small she's hard to find.

My brother's like a bumblebee,
So cute and soft and fluffy,
So small and precious,
With striped hair, thick and puffy.

Amber Daisy Collington (11)
Carrington Primary School

Summer's Here

Summer's here, let's all shout,
Children running all about,
Children scream, children shout,
The ice cream van is here,
Children run about, so they can get a cold ice cream,
Children running in the park to find a place so they can all be found,
People sitting on the ground,
There is singing and laughter all around,
Children swinging on the swing,
Children sliding on the slide,
And children playing in the sand,
People going for a picnic all around,
Summer's here, let's all shout,
Children running all about.

Samara Zahra Amjad (10)
Carrington Primary School

Seasons

Ah, springtime at last,
It took a while
But it came quite fast
It's the baby animals which make me smile
This year is gonna be a blast.

Yes, summer has begun
Ice cream sundae trickling down my throat
Lots of kids are having fun
Wow, look at those boats
I will give you a race there, but I won.

Boo, autumn is here
The leaves have gone mouldy and old
I've got a really bad fear
That I might get a bad cold
If I do, I will give it to someone near.

Brrr, winter is back, it's cold isn't it?
It has badly snowed
We've got to put on our hat, scarf and mitts
Every kid has just moaned
Because football is over, we can't keep fit.

Monique Price (11)
Carrington Primary School

The Caribbean Sea

The Caribbean Sea is a nice place to be
Just my family and me, under a coconut tree.

The Caribbean Sea is a fab place to be
Swimming in the warm, warm sea.

The Caribbean Sea is a cool place to be
Why don't you come and see.

The Caribbean Sea is a great place to be
Drinking rum under the great big sun.

Thomas Nattrass (8)
Cropwell Bishop Primary School

Winter

Winter feels evil
Like the Wicked Witch of the West
Casting a sinful spell on me

Winter feels bad
Like Jack Frost
Stealing all the warmth from me

Winter feels frosty
Scary and sad
Echoes of all the mean horrible things
That have happened in the past

Winter is ice
Thundering down
Icicles sharp as sharp can be
Snow falling
Falling like the Snow Queen in a dream
Melting down
Down
Deep down
Is this a dream . . . ?
Or a nightmare . . . ?
Winter.

Willow Richardson (8)
Cropwell Bishop Primary School

My Snowman

I look outside
And all is white.

I get on my wellies,
Which are rather smelly.

I run to make a snowman,
That looks like a postman.

I give him a hat,
That is very black.

Buttons for his eyes,
That shine in the light.

A carrot for his nose,
As long as a hose.

Sticks for his arms,
Like coconut palms.

I leave him there, in the cold,
Hoping he would not mould.

I go to bed very sleepy
I look outside
And he is weepy.

Matthew Ellis (7)
Cropwell Bishop Primary School

Stars

Stars twinkling bright,
Guiding us at night.
Stars lead our way
Every single day.

Stars led the kings
To angels on wings,
For it was Christmas
The birth of Jesus.

Stars keep on shining
Keeping us smiling.
Bright like a gem
Don't we just love them.

Starlight above,
Shine on those we love.
Reaching with arms,
To keep us from harm.

Emma Fear (7)
Cropwell Bishop Primary School

Hurricanes

House-wrecking hurricanes
Stormy, windy hurricanes
Blowing, flowing hurricanes
Coming to the town

Bashing, dashing hurricanes
Smashing, flashing hurricanes
Breaking, shaking hurricanes
Going through the town

Town-flattening hurricanes
Crushing, rushing hurricanes
Crashing, mashing hurricanes
Gone from the town.

Alicia Pears (8)
Cropwell Bishop Primary School

What Is A Snowflake?

A snowflake is the breath of a reindeer
While flying in the wind,

It is a chip off a crystal
Shimmering for Santa to find his way,

It is a diamond on a bracelet
From Santa for a Christmas present,

It is a chandelier
Glimmering by the fire,

It is a spirit's frozen soul
Coming down from the night sky.

Max Black (9)
Cropwell Bishop Primary School

There's A Snake In My Bed!

There's a snake in my bed!
I think he made me spill some ink.
Then he squiggled and swerved,
I got a nerve.
I shouted help,
Then I had to yelp.
But no one came,
Because they thought I was playing a game.
He struggled up and down,
Like a clown.
I jumped out of bed,
I grabbed my ted.
I ran downstairs,
I got some chairs.
Then climbed to the top,
But I wanted to pop.
I got the broom,
From the room.
I slammed the broom down,
On the snake's head.
That was the end of the snake in my bed!

Charlotte Price (9)
Cropwell Bishop Primary School

Winter

Winter, when the sun has gone
When white snow covers the land
When icicles glisten in the sky

Winter when life has disappeared
When scarves are brought
When the hot fire warms the house

Winter when Santa brings presents to good kids and coal to bad
When people kiss under holly
When a new year starts.

Elly Keal (9)
Cropwell Bishop Primary School

The Blue Starfish

There once was a starfish
Who was very swish.

He lived in the sea
And his name was Lee.

He was light and blue
And very chubby too.

He liked to drink wine
And he lived in the vines.

He had a girlfriend who was pink
Sometimes she made his heart sink.

She was very pretty
And had a pet called Kitty.

Whilst swimming around
They heard a loud sound.

They saw big teeth
Amongst the reef.

No more starfish in the sea
A great big shark has had them for tea.

Abigail Ellis (9)
Cropwell Bishop Primary School

The City Of Hell

Walking through the centre of this city,
It is dark - dark and dead.
Looking around me nothing here but lost souls,
Drifting through time and space.
I am a lost soul walking through the City of Hell.

Walking through the middle of this city,
It is cold - cold and dead.
Nothing but soft, distant echoes from long-lost souls,
Floating around past, present and future,
As I walk through the centre of Hell.

Walking into the centre of my destiny,
It is frightening - frightening and dead.
There is nothing but the deep fiery depths of Hell,
Scorching my skin and poisoning my heart,
As I walk through the centre of Hell.

Walking through the City of Hell,
It is evil - evil and dead.
All around me nothing but red light and orange smoke,
Burning my eyes and killing my body,
As I walk through the City of Hell.

Walking through the City of Death,
It is black - black and dead.
All around me nothing, no one . . . silence . . .
Suffocating me in my last seconds,
As I die in the *City of Hell*.

Georgina Taylor (10)
Cropwell Bishop Primary School

Flowers

Poppies are as red as lollipops
Sparkling in the light.
Lilies are as white as snow
Twinkling from Heaven.
Pansies are as purple as blackberry juice
Swirling in a bowl.
Sunflowers are as yellow as the sun
Shining in the blue sky.
Snapdragons are as pink as a newborn baby
Sleeping in her cot.

Caley Mayhew (10)
Cropwell Bishop Primary School

The Tooth Fairy

I fall into a deep sleep,
Dreaming on my pillow,
Dreaming of ice cream, blue skies
And toasted marshmallows.

And while I stay fast asleep,
Suddenly a flutter,
A pitter-patter of feet.

The tooth fairy is working her fairy magic,
Jumping high, jumping low,
Spinning fast, soaring low.

She takes my tooth,
She flies away,
She left a coin the very next day.

The tooth fairy rides on a boat,
Through the clouds
And gentle, but firm,
She places my tooth right into the sky,
Now I look out of my window
And look at the star
That's my tooth travelling afar.

Jessica Nattrass (10)
Cropwell Bishop Primary School

The Rainbow I Saw . . .

The rainbow I saw was gleaming
And protecting its colours
Like a guard and its treasure.
The rainbow I saw was standing still
Like a flower with no breeze.
The rainbow I saw was so beautiful
It was like falling into a heavenly dream.
The rainbow I saw made a colourful circle onto a lake
Like a merry-go-round but as still as a candle flame.
The rainbow I saw was like fairy dust
Scattered in the sky.
The rainbow I saw faded away
Like a dream I never had.

Emily Barratt (10)
Cropwell Bishop Primary School

Saturn

Sitting in her cave of darkness
Brightly lit by the sun,
Alas, she was dreaming
Eager for people to come.

She started to smile
Knowing one day
That she would get visitors
That will come to play.

So she started to change
Changing her atmosphere
From gas to oxygen
So people have nothing to fear.

But her eagerness bought her fate
A large rock came
Crashing into her
So now she'll have to reform again.

Katie Veasey (11)
Cropwell Bishop Primary School

I Speak My Very Last Word

I speak my very last word,
For my heart beats ever so slowly.
My life's gone down the drain,
My poor, unvalued existence,
Leaves me only in the anger of vain.

Take me to my bed of death,
The grave of which I will lie,
For over a thousand years,
I say my last goodbyes,
To those fears which disappoint me.

I speak my very last word,
For now I will go away.
To the high Heaven above,
Of which I will stay,
I speak my very last word.

Rebecca Denty (11)
Cropwell Bishop Primary School

Wishes

A dream in your pocket,
A wish in your shoe,
A rainbow to wear
And a moonbeam or two,
A smile on your face
And a star in your hair -
Hope today makes you feel . . .
Like you're walking on air!

Claudia Wright (8)
Cropwell Bishop Primary School

Gone

Like the sun with no shadow,
Like a mirror with no reflection,
Like a vibration with no sound,
Like a house with no lights,
Only me, missing you.

Andrew Johnson (10)
Hempshill Hall Primary School

Stuck In The Middle

Mum's running about, doing her best,
Niece is at the child minder's, wondering where the rest is,
Sister's out and about, getting depressed,
Not seen brother for a while, wonder how he's doing?
But I'm just stuck in the middle
Wondering what I should be doing.

Jerome Vernon-Day (10)
Hempshill Hall Primary School

Happy New Year

H appy New Year, it's come again
A dvent's over now - new beginning
P eople cheering
P eople rejoicing
Y ou are thinking - what shall I do?

N ew page to work on
E veryone starting afresh
W alking over past memories

Y early traditions - soon to come
E verybody noisily planning
A head of time
R esolutions, here we come!

Jessica Palmer (11)
Hempshill Hall Primary School

Football Crazy - Kennings

Football lover
Goal scorer
Accurate passer
Penalty taker

Offside hater
Hard worker
Celebration maker
Corner kicker

Water bottle drinker
Half-time refresher
Training liker
Winning striker

Red card never
Yellow card disliker
Sliding tackler
Rolls Royce forever!

Sam Hickman (10)
Hempshill Hall Primary School

The Calming Landscape

A waterfall making a slow
Soft trickling sound
Into a lake calm and still.
Way above the glittering mountain
The sky a rich blue
And beneath the dazzling sky,
Lay a forest, a shiny emerald-green
Beside the lake a bank of wild flowers lay,
In orange, yellow and green.

Leah Boughen (11)
Hempshill Hall Primary School

I Love You!

Loving you is right for me,
You're the best boy ever
And I want you to see.
My heart breaks when I'm all alone
But you come and cheer me up
Like I'm cosy at home.
I smile at you
You smile at me
I just hope this isn't a dream.

Louise Tokelove (11)
Hempshill Hall Primary School

Are You My Valentine?

It's Valentine's Day
And I want you to know
You're the best boy ever
And I love you so

'Cause you're the best boy
I have recognised
If only you'll be by my side

You're sweet, you're kind
And are you mine?
So please baby, please be my valentine!

You're sweet, you're kind
And are you mine?
So please baby, please be my valentine!

Natalie Bennett & Leah Boughen (11)
Hempshill Hall Primary School

Valentine's Day

It's Valentine's Day
And I tell you so,
You're the cutest boy,
I'll ever know.

You are so kind,
You are so sweet,
You're the nicest boy,
I'll ever meet.

You are so clean,
You sparkle and shine,
On this special day
Be my valentine
Will you be mine?

So I want you to know,
At this romantic time,
I want you to be,
My valentine!

Rebecca Louise Brudenell (10)
Hempshill Hall Primary School

Time Machine

If I had a time machine
I could go to the year 3,000,
Just imagine all the flying cars and trams.
Or I can go to 1 BC,
Just imagine all the caves and cavemen.
Then choose which one I like best,
Probably the year 3,000
But I like it just at the year that it is now.
Just perfect!

Joshua Furby (10)
Hempshill Hall Primary School

Magic Box

(Based on 'Magic Box' by Kit Wright)

In my box I will put . . .
Posh ladies dancing to funny music
And my most exciting dreams that I will keep.

In my box I will put . . .
A diving dolphin sweeping through the sea
And all my happy feelings from the past.

In my box I will put . . .
Mad bunnies hopping through the long grass
And the best family anyone would want.

In my box I will put . . .
All my hopes that I share
And all four seasons that spread such fun.

In my box I will put . . .
The first Christmas of the world
And blossoming spring flowers that shoot up from the ground.

In my box I will put . . .
My birthday when I was four
And my very first tooth from when I was so small.

In my box I will put . . .
The very first Easter egg I ever saw
And falling autumn leaves in different shades of brown.

But most of all I will put my lovely memories from the past
I think my box is very full, so now I will put the lid on it
I shall look in my box another day,
So until then, I will keep my box very close to me.

Ellie Batey (8)
Leen Mills Primary School

The Wind Is . . .

The wind is a dog howling,
Paws as big as the Earth,
His bark is as loud as an earthquake,
His body fur tangled
And sticking up,
His ears twice as big
As an elephant's,
His large tail sweeping one side of the Earth,
His howl crossing the other.

Sarah Stevenson (10)
Leen Mills Primary School

What's Green?

Green is a leaf
Dangling on a branch
Green is a snake
Gliding through the grass
Green is a lake
Shimmering across the water
Green is an apple
Being picked from a tree
Green is a candle
The flames dancing around
Green is grass
Blowing in the breeze
Green is a frog
Jumping to a lily pad
Green is a podded pea
Delicious and sweet to eat
Green is cabbage
Stood on its own
Green is a lime
Sat in a bowl.

Ashleigh Walters (10)
Leen Mills Primary School

Fairy

I have never seen a fairy,
So I do not really know,
But if I saw a fairy,
This is how it would go . . .

I think she is all sparkly,
Her wings are see-through,
A sweet little nose and a sweet little mouth,
Her eyes are lovely and blue.

Her hair is blonde and silky,
Light and delicate, she glides through the sky,
Her body is slim with a rose petal dress,
She flies through the sky like a butterfly.

She's kind and gentle all the time,
She looks after children all night,
She scares away monsters,
She stops them having a fright!

You never know, one day you might be lucky
And see a fairy on a toadstool,
I would love to see a magical fairy,
It would be very *cool!*

Emily Parkes (8)
Leen Mills Primary School

Hucknall Town

Really slow, in a traffic jam,
People walking with babies in prams.
Ten miles per hour, I'm watching the clock,
I wish I was outside, shopping at Peacocks.

I'm so hungry, seeing fish and chips,
I'm sitting here, licking my lips.
Passing Thorntons, my favourite shop,
I hope we can stop and buy a chocolate lollipop.

I see my friends, meeting at Martins,
They all come out with a packet of Smarties.
Someone help! My mum won't let me go,
Because she's taking us both to bingo!

Molly Strawson (11)
Leen Mills Primary School

My Hippie Grandmother

This is all about my grandma, Annie G
She's someone who I would like to be.
She used to wear high-heeled shoes
And a bag to match
And the boys used to think
She was a wonderful catch!
She married Grandad
And she became his
After a year
They had four kids!
Annie G had six grandchildren
I was number six
There are three great-grandchildren on the way
Makes her feel like 106!

Holly Goodall (8)
Leen Mills Primary School

My Puppy, The Pain

I have a puppy, his name is Shane,
He runs around and he's a real big *pain!*
So I chuck him out in the rain,
I let him in, he's still the same!

So I give him a hug,
I give him love
And my little puppy
Goes *woof, woof, woof!*

And that's my poem of my little pup!

Ria Anderson (9)
Leen Mills Primary School

My Uncle

I have an uncle called Wayne
He goes to work all day
But I think he just goes to play
He come home at six
And smells just like the pits!

He sits down for his tea
But then he needs a wee
He has sausage and chips
And it goes to his hips!

He goes to the gym
To try and build some muscles
But what he really needs
Is to eat lots of Brussels!

My uncle comes from Blackpool
Which is really cool
And I love him lots and lots
Just like my favourite Jelly Tots!

Amy Butt (7)
Leen Mills Primary School

In My Wonderful Box

(Inspired by 'Magic Box' by Kit Wright)

In my wonderful box I would put in my fascinating Lego,
In my wonderful box I would put in all my brilliant creations,
In my wonderful box I would put in all my friends,
In my wonderful box I would put in my great cubs,
In my wonderful box I would put in my neat hopes,
In my wonderful box I would put in my kindness,
Now I think I should close my box, as it is full to the top!

Lewis Bryce Humphreys (9)
Leen Mills Primary School

Grandpa's Garden

In Grandpa's garden I can see,
Pretty purple pansies,
Super yellow sunflowers,
Dazzling white daisies.

In Grandpa's garden I can smell,
Sweet aromas of rose,
Sensational perfumes of lilies,
Perfect fragrances of freesias.

In Grandpa's garden I can hear,
Sweet songbirds chirping softly,
Tiny baby mice squeaking quietly,
Next-door's dog growling loudly.

In Grandpa's garden I can feel,
The wind blowing gently on my face,
Green grass tickling my bare feet
And warming rays of sunshine on my skin.

125 Park Road East,
My favourite place to be,
With Nanna and Grandpa too,
It's Heaven on Earth for me!

Megan Unwin (11)
Leen Mills Primary School

Rainbows

Rainbows are colourful
Rainbows are cheerful
Rainbows are really relaxing
Rainbows are peaceful
Rainbows glide through the sky
Rainbows can fly and reach up high for the sky
Have you seen a rainbow fly?
Because I haven't
Have you?

Chloe Allen (8)
Leen Mills Primary School

In My World

Smile, beautiful,
Palm tree, tall and strong,
Islands, full of life,
Christmas, joyful,
Sheep, shy and scared,
The past, unstoppable,
The future, untouchable,
Moments, heart-stopping,
My life, my hopes,
My dreams, my world.

Brody Asher (9)
Leen Mills Primary School

In My Box

(Based on 'Magic Box' by Kit Wright)

In my precious box I will put . . .
The air that's all around us
The amazing fun we have in there.
I will put my nice games that are cool
In my box, my box of niceness,
I will put my friends and cousins.
In my box I will keep my mum, dad, sister
And my life.
In my box I will put a frog
And the Lord.
My box, covered in diamonds, rubies too
I will keep a toy car, toy aeroplane
My Airfix model as well and a toy Spitfire.
In my box will be Robin Hood
And lots of words.
In my box will be my imagination.

Callum Boorman (8)
Leen Mills Primary School

In My Box

(Based on 'Magic Box' by Kit Wright)

In my box I will put . . .
My guinea pig squealing
My helpful best friends

I will put in my box . . .
Proper caring family
Sharing kindness

In my box I will put . . .
Food to live and be healthy
Water so we don't dehydrate

I will put in my box . . .
Living, free animals
And sweet dreams

In my box I will put . . .
World peace with no wars
Spreading joy around the universe

I will put in my box . . .
The biggest, brightest light
Doctors to cure people

In my box I will put . . .
Intelligent teachers
Great helpers
And my life.

Joanne Heathcote (8)
Leen Mills Primary School

In My Box

(Inspired by on 'Magic Box' by Kit Wright)

In my box I'll put in big woolly wolves that I like
In my box I'll put in my kindness for life
In my box I'll put in my happiness all the time
In my box I'll put in bricks of Lego to build
In my box I'll put in a piece of moon for light
In my box I'll put in a piece of sun for heat
In my box I'll put in my friends to play
In my box I'll put in a toy plane for fun
In my box I'll put in a book to read for a long time
In my box I'll put in hopes hoping it will stop raining
In my box I'll put in my gratefulness to help other people before myself
In my box I'll put in my favourite pens to write poems with
In my box I'll put in my Cub badges to remind me
How hard I've worked.

Alex Michael Chadwick (8)
Leen Mills Primary School

In My Class Today

Map learning,
Chair squirming,
Chess playing,
Children praying,
Book reading,
Puzzle succeeding,
Number crunching,
Apple munching,
Paint splodging,
Ball dodging,
Coat grabbing,
Scarf flapping,
Mums coming,
Boys running

And that was my day at school.

Edward Turner (9)
Leen Mills Primary School

Numbers Are Fun!

Do some counting every day,
It's a clever way to play,
Numbers are fun, so count with me,
Let's start slowly, one, two, three.

Count the flowers by the gate,
Count the peas upon your plate,
Count the ducklings near a boat,
Count the buttons on your coat.

Two bright eyes,
One little nose,
How many fingers?
How many toes?

Keep it easy, one, two, three, four,
As I get bigger, add some more.
If we do counting as I grow,
What big numbers I will know!

Siân Hudson (10)
Leen Mills Primary School

Always

The grass will always be green,
The sky will always be blue,
The river will always flow
And tomorrow will always be new.

The moon will always glisten,
The sun will always shine
And the stars in the jet-black sky
Will always be divine!

Phoebe-Lois Brown (10)
Leen Mills Primary School

What Is Red?

Red is a poppy,
Swaying in a battlefield.
Red is a rose,
Filled with lots of love.
Red is a fire,
Sitting in a fireplace.
Red is a butterfly,
Flying in the breezy sky.
Red is a jumper,
To keep you warm in the winter.
Red is a shiny tomato,
Sitting in a salad bowl.
Red is a sunset,
Sinking on the wavy sea.

Katy Bramley (9)
Leen Mills Primary School

In My Box

(Based on 'Magic Box' by Kit Wright)

In my box I will put a dolphin splashing in water
In my box I will put Fred bear
In my box I will put naughty little squirrels
In my box I will put a shy shark
In my box I will put a kind teacher
In my box I will put my imaginary friend
But most importantly, I will put my kindness and hopes.

Hazel Surgey (7)
Leen Mills Primary School

My Dolphin And Me

My dolphin is fab
It really is pretty
Everyone adores my dolphin
Especially me.
It flies through the waves
And floats through the sea.
It's pretty in sight
Flying through the waves
As pretty as can be.
So everyone adores my dolphin
Especially me!

Hannah Elson (7)
Leen Mills Primary School

In My Box

(Inspired by 'Magic Box' by Kit Wright)

In my box I can see
Sharp-toothed shark coming after me
In my box I can see
Diving dolphins splashing in the water
In my box I can see
Freaky fish blowing bubbles
In my box I can see
Roaring lions snoozing in their cages
In my box I can see
Rabbits playing under a tree
In my box I can see
Dazzling dogs chewing my toys
In my box I can see
A tortoise plodding along
In my box I can see
A crocodile snapping his teeth
In my box I can see
A cuddly teddy bear (cute!)
In my box I can see
My friendship that I share with my friends
In my box I can see
A cute kitten chasing after a cute dog
In my box I can see
A duck floating across the blue sea
In my box I can see
A nipping crab (I've never seen a crab)
And now I'm going to put in my cares and dreams
And now close the lid.

Hollie Bidwell (7)
Leen Mills Primary School

Starlight

Starlight, star bright
Stars twinkle every night
Astronauts are on the moon
But will they be home soon?
Lots of clouds are in the sky
Now everyone is saying goodbye.

Natalie Walpole (8)
Leen Mills Primary School

Life Without My Nintendo

Life without my Nintendo, what would it be?
Reading books and magazines
And watching boring old TV
Playing games is so much fun
As I complete the levels one by one
My Nintendo has some wonderful games
The one about dogs is my favourite
Making them sit, making them stand
Making them lie on my command.

Abigail Louise Wright (9)
Leen Mills Primary School

The Moonlight

The moonlight is a silver figure,
Walking across the moonlit sky.
The moonlight is a silent lady,
Dodging through the wood.
The moonlight is a gazing star,
Watching over us.
The moonlight is a quiet lady,
Gliding across the garden.
The moonlight is a silver river,
With still, silver fish.
The moonlight is a tree,
With silver apples and pears on it.

Jessica Southall (10)
Leen Mills Primary School

The River

The river is a snake
Trailing towards the sea.
He shakes his tail
As he goes around the curvy corner.
He crashes around
Making a horrible noise.
It sounds like he's angry.
He's almost there.
What can he see?
The deep blue sea.

Eleanor Boultby (10)
Leen Mills Primary School

The Beach

Children eating huge ice creams,
Bursting all their swimwear seams
All the elders sitting in the shade,
Slurping down their Lucozade
It's so hot, everyone's burning, we could use a fan,
Ladies trying not to move, to get their perfect tan
Men are digging in the boiling sand,
While babies annoy the seaside's band
It's time to go, so pack up your things and put them in the car,
I'm afraid to say, I've had enough, it's time to say ta-ta!

Cara Williams (10)
Leen Mills Primary School

Crazy Football

There is a footballer called Pele
You see him lots on the telly
When he has the ball
He dribbles them all
And the goalkeeper's legs turn to jelly.

Bradley Perkins (8)
Leen Mills Primary School

My Dreams

My dream is to become a marine biologist,
My dream is to live in the sea,
My dream is to look after sea animals,
My dream is to see what they see,
My dream is to swim with them,
My dream is to become a marine biologist
So let me dream.

Hayley Goodwin (9)
Leen Mills Primary School

One Scary Night

One scary night, I lay in my bed,
Listening to the wind howling,
Trees tapping,
Ghosts moaning,
Bats flapping,
Doors creaking,
Floorboards squeaking,
While I shivered in fright.

Leanne Creasey (11)
Leen Mills Primary School

My Shiny Teeth

My shiny teeth are as shiny as can be
Cleaned in the morning
Floss every day after my tea
Cleaned in the evening
My shiny teeth are as shiny as can be.

Daniel Wright (9)
Leen Mills Primary School

Together

Boys
Stinky, rough
Giggling, kicking, nagging
Football, Action Man, pretty and careful
Shopping, hopping, dancing
Understanding, wishful
Girls.

Katrina Ellingworth (8)
Leen Mills Primary School

Butterfly Garden

Excuse me, excuse me,
But I can't get to my
Beautiful butterfly garden.

You must have seen it,
You must have seen it,
It is full of gorgeous flowers
And bright coloured birds,
My beautiful butterfly garden.

I've seen it, I've seen it,
It's right over there,
Under that rainbow
And next to the deep blue sea,
Your beautiful butterfly garden.

Sarah Titterton (8)
Leen Mills Primary School

My Dog, Chester

We've got a dog called Chester,
For short we just call him Chest
Although he is a bit of a nuisance,
We still think he is the best!
Chester has brown eyes and a brown nose,
On top of his head, his hair is all curly
Sometimes his hair is scruffy
And other times, it's twirly.
We love Chester, we really do,
He is so cute.
So sometimes he even brings our shoe,
Sometimes he is very wise.
Chest loves to eat anything, like:
Turkey and carrots.
Well, anything really, but he absolutely loves pies!

Hannah Collis (10)
Leen Mills Primary School

The Little Star

The man in the moon, he blinked one eye,
When the little star began to cry.
A happy little cloud then came along,
Singing a very merry song.
Everything then was quite alright
And the little star twinkled all through the night.

Eleanor Gladman (8)
Leen Mills Primary School

My Puppy

My puppy is called Toto,
He is very tame and when you call his name
He will hop for fun and his mum,
Toto, Toto, what a beautiful name,
Toto he runs around your garden day and night.

Elise Diamond Radford (8)
Leen Mills Primary School

My Magic Box

(Inspired by 'Magic Box' by Kit Wright)

In my box I will put . . .
My wicked Nintendo DS
In my box I will put . . .
By best CD player
In my box I will put . . .
My old snowman
In my box I will put . . .
My special personality
In my box I will put . . .
My darkest secrets
In my box I will put . . .
My wild imagination
In my box I will put . . .
My best ever television
In my box I will put . . .
My good happiness
In my box I will put . . .
My gloomy sadness
In my box I will put . . .
My favourite DVDs and videos
In my box I will put . . .
My first teddy
In my box I will put . . .
My great pens and pencils
In the future there will be
Lots, lots more, but for now
That is enough!

Eleanor Bunting (8)
Leen Mills Primary School

Pestful Birds

Brand new Ferrari,
big flock of birds,
one gives a smirk,
plop! Dad's not happy.

What's that high in the sky?
Is it a bird?
Is it a plane?
No but it is loaded.

Dad got a shotgun,
not very happy,
ready to shoot.
Bang! Sorry birdie!

Ethan Thrower (9)
Leen Mills Primary School

Sun Poem

The sun shoots up her fiery rays
She heats the Earth with her bright gaze
She cuddles Earth and keeps it safe and warm
Keeps us away from the frightening storm
The rays shoot up like a gun being fired
The scorching heat makes us tired

The sun tans the world below
Until all the clouds deliver snow
Her smile always forgiving us
Higher than the clouds above
Her rays glimmer
With a beautiful shimmer

As round as a juicy peach
We can't go too close to the heat
Her lovely orange light
Disappears at night
She comes out every day
Also frightening night away.

Georgia Barrowcliffe (10)
Redlands Primary School

Sun

The golden sun is so bright
Just like a shining star at night
She looks down on us
To keep us warm

Our circular sun
When it rains
We are all sad
But when the sun comes out we'll be glad

When the night comes
We get in bed
Close your eyes
There will be a surprise
To see a beautiful sun again.

Lauren Morris (10)
Redlands Primary School

The Sun

The sun rises
And shines upon the Earth,
With its glittering sparks,
As the world spins round in its glory,
Like a football rising into the air
Which has been kicked to the back of a net.

The sun shines,
Down on the Earth,
Spreading its light far and wide
Across the globe,
Dazzling people with its bright shine,
Heating up our planet.

The sun shines on a summer's day,
Children playing in icy pools,
Licking their melting lollipops,
While the sun burns down on them.

Jake Milson & Jordanna Williams (10)
Redlands Primary School

Sun Poem

Sun, sun as sweet as a bun,
As round as a cherry,
As sweet as a berry,
Sun, sun as sweet as a bun.

Sun, sun delightful as a cuddle,
You dry up the rain puddle,
Your calming heat,
Shines way up in the sky.

Sun, sun your golden rays,
Brighten up our darkest days,
You get us out of our bed,
Calling, 'Come on, get up, you sleepy head!'

Emma Tuke (10) & Bethany Roberts (11)
Redlands Primary School

The Sun

The sun shoots up its fiery rays,
Heats the Earth with its bright gaze.

The sun cuddles Earth and keeps it safe and warm,
Keeps us from the frightening storm.

It tans the world below,
Until all the clouds deliver snow.

The colour's like an orange, the shape's like a ball,
It stands in the sky, so bright and tall.

Like a bulb, it brightens the moon,
So at night we have some light.

Ainsley Kirk (11)
Redlands Primary School

Sun Poem

She is a child trampling in a strop,
She shines like a light bulb with a luminescent glow,
She floats in the sky all the way to the top,
She is a giant tennis ball going with the flow.

If she approaches you, you will burn,
She flips to moon at night,
In the dark, she will turn,
But in the day, she is so bright.

Great, gigantic, yellow ball gleaming,
You're as sweet as music from a cello,
Your shine is so beaming,
Oh great sun, 'Hello!'

Victoria Johnson & Lewis Linacre (10)
Redlands Primary School

Sun Poem

The golden sun,
As round as a football,
The golden nugget high in the sky
Before your very eyes,
Sun, sun you're so fun
The gleaming sun makes light for us
Everywhere we look
Sun, sun you're as round as a bun.

Nathan Chambers (11)
Redlands Primary School

Sun

Sun, sun, you are so fun!
You're as blinding as a torch
And as shiny as a sequin,
Sun, sun, you are so fun!

You have millions of fiery rays
And a beautiful smile upon your face,
Your beams are so bright,
Like a silver star in the night.

You drift around so gracefully,
Staring brightly down on me,
Making me feel so dreamy,
Sun, sun, you are so fun!

Bayley Pimperton-Vergeldt & Jessie Gilham (10)
Redlands Primary School

Sun Poem

The sun is as yellow as a melon,
Floating in the air,
The rays shine across the sky,
Like bright yellow hair.

She is as round as a football,
Tanning all the trees,
She's as hot as a gas oven,
She makes people sweat, especially their knees.

Smiling sun makes happier faces,
Cuddling the world below,
She is as round as a pizza
And as bright as a night light,
So now it's night, let's turn off this bright light.

Nathan Singleton (11)
Redlands Primary School

The Sun

The sun is seeming to be gleaming on a summer's day,
The lightness and the brightness is shining on your way,
Heat is like a fiery diary full of secrets, waiting to unfold,
It is far too precious to be sold.

The rooster awakes everyone in the morn,
The farms are in their fields gathering their corn,
The sun travels the world day and night,
Its golden rays shining so bright.

Travelling from New York to Hong Kong,
The blackbird is singing his song,
As golden as a ring,
As round as a ball,
The sun is looking down at us all.

Ashlie Kelly & Chloe Pressley (11)
Redlands Primary School

Sun

The sun's like a gold diamond ring,
As bright as a star in the night sky,
As warm as a cuddle,
As sweet as an orange,
The sun's like a gold diamond ring.

The sun is circular in a shape of a bun,
It glistens and gleams and sparkles like a gun,
It stares at you in the morning,
It stares at you in the night,
Like a very, very bright light.

Like a breath of warm air against your face,
Like a ball of fire that's in a race,
As red as cherries,
As ripe as berries,
As sweet as a flower where the honeybees buzz.

Laura Harwin (11) & Danielle Dickinson (10)
Redlands Primary School

The Sun

Up it comes, higher and higher,
Towering above like a roaring fire.
Gazing down from his throne of clouds,
As he makes his way round and round.

Destroys the night, but creates the light,
As he creeps from his long sleep.
As round as a football in all his pride,
Close to the moon, he swims and glides.

Shining light from fiery red beams,
Gives the planet that glowing gleam.
Lighter of the Earth, king of the day,
Shows the world the right way.

The sun!

The most powerful flame,
The thing that no fireman can ever tame!

Megan Berridge & Elinor Brophy (11)
Redlands Primary School

The Sun

Obliterating the moon's light
And the sun peers down onto Earth,
In its fireball of glory
Kids come out and play in the sunlight
Eating ice cream.

The sun was as light as a buttercup flower
Absorbing some power, power, power.

Now it's time for the sun to go
Away even further
Through the cold winter snow.

Lawrence Mitchell (11) & Ross Prince (10)
Redlands Primary School

The Sun

The sun shines high up in the sky
But nobody seems to care
He runs along the sky each day
Moving here and there.

Where you see him
High up there
You're bound to clap and cheer
And when we go to bed
You'll still be there.

When you watch us
Throughout the day
And when we're lost
You show the way.

Alicia Kirkland (11)
Redlands Primary School

Sun Poem

The sun, the sun, is a yellow gas ball,
Like a sunflower gleaming in the sky.
High, high, high, higher every day,
Smiling all the way, making children play.

Golden disco light sparkling everywhere,
Sparkle, sparkle, all glittery.
Shine upon the world,
Make it light once again.

Flowers growing strength in the earth,
Bright and early gleam once more,
Make it shine,
Once and for all.

Gabrielle Lee (10) & Chloe Schofield (11)
Redlands Primary School

Sun

Silently the sun rises into the day,
Brighter than mankind can say.
It lights the Earth with its almighty powers,
Concealed above in its mighty tower.

Glowing golden throughout the day,
Very special in every way.
Like a mother to the world,
As a guidance to us all.
Her powerful eye and her fiery rays,
Bring back our summer days.

Like a cuddle she gives us heat,
Could cook plenty for us to eat.
Like a fiery flame,
The sun is shining again.

Alex Cooke & Connah-Marie Locke (10)
Redlands Primary School

Sun

The sun is as round as a table tennis ball,
As it shines over the walls
And across the Atlantic ocean,
It is like a magic potion.

The sun gives all its powers,
It is higher than thirty towers,
As the sun goes higher and higher,
It slowly travels by the hour.

Laura Reed (10) & Ashley Lacey (11)
Redlands Primary School

The Sun

The sun is a fire that no man can extinguish,
It strolls the day until darkness roars.
It is as blinding as the core of Earth,
The sun is as boiling as a rocket taking off,
Every new day the sun is reborn.

The sun is as bright as the lightest torch,
It is as hot as chilli sauce.
The sun is as round as a big tennis ball,
But mainly of all it is so tall.

The sun is a lemon for its big, bright colour,
It is more scolding than leaking acid,
While the sun is here, you will have no fear.

Nathan Owen & Oliver Pingree (10)
Redlands Primary School

Sun Poem

The sun is shining out today, hip hip hooray!
The sun reflects off the pond,
As she waves her powerful wand,
When she moves along the sky,
It's like she is flying.

The sun gleams over the land,
As children run over her sand,
The blinding sun looks upon the woolly clouds.

As the sun shines her golden light,
She puts up her fight,
To stop the rain peaking through.

Children playing,
The sun draining,
Here we go, hip hip hooray!

Jade Duckmanton (10)
Redlands Primary School

The Glimmering Sun

Slowly glimmering upon the rustling trees,
The sun galloping along the galaxy,
As round as a football
And we can see it all,
One by one it rises upon another rustling tree.

The sun's glimmering shine will blind anyone,
But still weighs a tonne,
Hip hip hooray, the sun has come out to play,
High, high, so high, no one dares to go so high.

The sun is like a hot air balloon rising,
Across the glimmering moon,
As it's rising, it looks as if it's a fireball,
Coming to us all, all, all.

Jamie Park (10)
Redlands Primary School

Grandad

(This poem is dedicated to my grandad Bob, who sadly passed away on 16th January 2006)

You need your grandad when you're feeling sad
You tell him your troubles and he says they're just like bubbles
They burst and don't leave a trace but you can tell by my face
That it is all going wrong, so he sings me a song
And he does that wrong, but you've got to admit
That as he worked down the pit
You need your grandad when you're feeling sad.

Sheridan Proctor (11)
Redlands Primary School

The Sun

Up high in the sky,
She sits on her throne,
A queen of summer in gold.

She's a bright light
And brings our holidays,
Round and round in just one day.

She's a ball of heat,
Who keeps us warm
And will be back in the coming morn.

Connah-Marie Locke (10)
Redlands Primary School

My Friend, Clara

My friend, Clara, is really nice
She welcomes everyone new
She always checks everything twice
She really likes dumpling stew
She's really friendly
She's nothing like me and you
She's smart and clever
And her boots are made of leather
Clara has been my best friend for years
And she really, really cares.

Keri-Anne Harrison (9)
St Margaret Clitherow RC Primary School, Bestwood Park

I've Got Night Fever

I've got night fever,
I just become a diva,
I can't help my feet,
Dancing to the beat.
I just prance around,
Leaping off the ground,
I just become a diva,
When I've got night fever!

Clara Dunphy (10)
St Margaret Clitherow RC Primary School, Bestwood Park

Hallowe'en

H is for horror
A is for alien
L is for little skeletons
L is for lonely souls
O ld witches
W itches' brew
E xtraordinary costumes
E xtraordinary ghost trains
N obody walks around at night.

Rosie Blyton Flewitt (9)
St Margaret Clitherow RC Primary School, Bestwood Park

My Family

My sister is loud
And she is very proud.
My brother is mean
And whenever something gets broken
He is never seen.
My cousin is small
And likes to play ball.

Callum Asher (10)
St Margaret Clitherow RC Primary School, Bestwood Park

My Uncle Bob

My uncle Bob he's a real slob
He picks his nose
At fancy shows.
He sings in the shower
He gets louder and louder
And he weeps.
To be honest I think
He's a total creep!

Sinead Shaw (9)
St Margaret Clitherow RC Primary School, Bestwood Park

Wrestling

W is for wicked
R is for Raw
E is for elimination chamber
S is for Smackdown
T is for tornado tag
L is for ladder
I is for the Irish Finlay
N is for never-ending wrestling
G is for grappling.

Curtis Kilcullen (9)
St Margaret Clitherow RC Primary School, Bestwood Park

Football

Football is great,
I play with my mates.
On the pitch where we play,
People scream, cheer and shout, 'Hooray!'
Tackling is what we do best,
It's hard to be a ref.
By the time the match ends,
We still should be friends.
We've all had great fun,
We are proud of what we've done,
Football is great!

Jack Northridge (9)
St Margaret Clitherow RC Primary School, Bestwood Park

The World

The world is round and blue
The world is big and wide too
The world has different countries
That everyone can visit
Oh, the world is so big
I like the world very much.

Bamu Fru (10)
St Margaret Clitherow RC Primary School, Bestwood Park

My Big Sister

Let me tell you about my big sister,
But so she doesn't hear
I will have to whisper.

She sneaks in my room and takes some of my things
I know when she does it
Because she always sings.

When I ask her why she goes in
The things she comes up with,
I don't know where to begin!

Jessica Carney (9)
St Margaret Clitherow RC Primary School, Bestwood Park

Irish Dancing Is The Best

Irish dancing is the best
Irish dancing is a test
I have not won
But tried a tonne
Irish dancing is the best!

Caitlin Wall (8)
St Margaret Clitherow RC Primary School, Bestwood Park

Golf

Golf, with ball and club, is great to play
Outside, in the fresh air, walking all day,
Landing in a bunker full of sand,
For it is not a very good place to land.

Connor Hopkins (9)
St Margaret Clitherow RC Primary School, Bestwood Park

Ikeido

I is for ideas
K is for karate
E is for eyes
I is for Ikeido
D is for do
O is for obvious.

Holly Chapman (10)
St Margaret Clitherow RC Primary School, Bestwood Park

Pterodactyl

My pterodactyl gives me a ride
High in the air.
He has short brown legs
And lumbers along.

He hunts like an eagle
Stalking his prey.
He swoops down to the sea
And snaps up a fish.

He flies out over the sea
Looking for dinner.
He flies back to his nest
To feed his precious young.

Jareth Evens (10)
St Margaret Clitherow RC Primary School, Bestwood Park

On My Way To School

Today I met a lion,
On my way to school.
Its mane was very hot
And it paws were rather cool.
I hid him in my satchel,
So the teacher would not see.
He sat there very quietly,
Till frightened by a bee!

Enya Powell (10)
St Margaret Clitherow RC Primary School, Bestwood Park

Walking To School

Whilst my mum was driving me to school,
I was thinking that I could walk because school's not far.
So the next time, I was allowed to walk to school,
Instead of wasting all that fuel.

I took big steps whilst walking to school,
I was fit and healthy when I reached school,
I could have swum for hours in a swimming pool.

I looked at my watch to see the time,
I had a quick jog, it wasn't a crime,
Feeling fit and healthy I made my way,
Singing songs with the birds, oh what a beautiful day!

Kyra Foster (11)
St Margaret Clitherow RC Primary School, Bestwood Park

Excuses, Excuses

'I couldn't do my homework, Miss Cooling,
I had asthma and was wheezing,
I had nosebleeds, measles, heat rash
And some very annoying sneezing.

My skin was itchy and had blisters,
Oh so blotchy red, hivy,
Toothaches in my mouth
And spots from poisoned ivy.

Eight ant bites and hair loss
And a broken leg with scabies,
Rocky mountain spotted fever
And a case of rabies.

I really suffered, it was awful,
But I'm better now,
Could I have done my homework?
Not really, I don't see how!'

Rianna Skeete (11)
St Margaret Clitherow RC Primary School, Bestwood Park

Horse Crackers

Crackers was a horse,
I rode her on a course,
She wanted to trot,
But got her hoof stuck in a slot.

She cantered along,
Neighing a song,
The ride was bumpy,
The saddle was lumpy.

Crackers did stumble,
So I began to mumble,
She nearly flattened a dog
And jumped over a log.

It was really quite fun,
To feel the horse run,
When we had to go home, I was sad
And Crackers went mad.

Rosie Burke (10)
St Margaret Clitherow RC Primary School, Bestwood Park

My First Day At School

Here is something that sticks in my mind,
It was when I found someone that was kind,
It was my first day at school,
When I heard about it, I wanted to drool,
I went on my way,
On my very special day.

I was crying, I was mad,
I was really, really sad,
When we got there, my mum left,
I could do nothing, so I wept.

I was there for a while, it was a long wait,
Someone came up to me, I found out it was Nate,
The day was really nice,
In fact, it went in a trice.

By the end of the day,
I went on my way,
The very next time,
We had to write words that rhyme,
I had a fabulous time,
Writing this rhyme.

Bill Dallman (10)
St Margaret Clitherow RC Primary School, Bestwood Park

Arsenal

I like football
Because of Henry
He makes football seem so great to me
The way he does all his skills and scores goals
I wonder if his foot is made out of gold?

Andre Skeete (7)
St Margaret Clitherow RC Primary School, Bestwood Park

My Little Lion

My little lion has sharp teeth and he likes to bite on meat,
He likes his lioness because she is the best,
As he soars through the jungle, he usually roars,
He wants to have a bite, but he often has a fright,
He is hunting through the jungle, it makes his tummy rumble,
His claws are sharp, always cutting through the bark,
But he is good in some kind of way, creeping slowly every day.

Ama Fru (8)
St Margaret Clitherow RC Primary School, Bestwood Park

Learning To Read

At first, all I could do
Was look at books
I then began my ABC
I then became a scheme reader
And now I am a free reader
Hip hip hooray!

Shola Thomas-Lewis (7)
St Margaret Clitherow RC Primary School, Bestwood Park

The Garden Fairies

I like little fairies
They're very small and neat
I see them in the garden
Sitting on the seat

They run amongst the flowers
Playing hide-and-seek
I creep down the garden
To have a little peek.

Lucy Smith (8)
St Margaret Clitherow RC Primary School, Bestwood Park

Taylor

T elly addict, that is me
A nyone's friend I will be
Y ou always say
L et's go and play
O thers say I'm very kind
R especting others, I do not mind.

Taylor Wright (7)
St Margaret Clitherow RC Primary School, Bestwood Park

Snow

There was some fluffy snow outside
Tip-tap-tapping on my window
I went outside to play
It made my teeth chit-chat-chatter
Building snowmen is so much fun
Carrot nose and coal for eyes
Pompom scarf and woolly hat
Time for tea and a nice warm bath
There was some fluffy snow outside
Tip-tap-tapping on my window.

Shannon Gaskell-Henson (8)
St Margaret Clitherow RC Primary School, Bestwood Park

My Friend, Sonny

My friend, Sonny, is really funny,
He makes me laugh when he's around,
He cheers me up when I feel down.

Sometimes we go camping,
We're always laughing.
We've been to Ireland,
You couldn't find a finer friend!

Sam Chapman (7)
St Margaret Clitherow RC Primary School, Bestwood Park

Hallowe'en

H aunted houses
A ll the children dressed up
L onely souls
L ittle skeletons
O ld people playing tricks
W itches' brews
E xciting ghost trains
E normous houses
N o one around in the silence of the night!

Olivia Davy-Hoffman (10)
St Margaret Clitherow RC Primary School, Bestwood Park

School

S is for school, we come here five days a week
C is for class, everyone works in one
H is for hall which we have assemblies in
O is for oboe, which is a musical instrument
O is for omelette, we have it at school dinner
L is for lovely, some of the teachers are
   That spells *school!*

Rebecca Joynt (9)
St Margaret Clitherow RC Primary School, Bestwood Park

Anger

Anger is a monster sleeping in my bed
Anger is a raging volcano
Anger looks like red flames
Anger tastes like hot flames.

Dylan Blake (8)
Sneinton CE Primary School

Love Is Like

Love is like a heart pumping
A fairy flying
Love smells like a blossom blowing softly in the wind and flowers
Love is the colour pink and purple
Love reminds me of my dog
Love, love, love!

Jade Mary Clarke (9)
Sneinton CE Primary School

Snow, Snow, Snow

Snow, snow, snow, it's coming too slow,
Snow, snow, snow, it's hard to blow,
Snow, snow, snow, it's just below,
Snow, snow, snow, it's so low,
Snow, snow, snow, it's underneath the show.

Snow, snow, snow, it really does glow,
Snow, snow, snow, it gives no path through the crow,
Snow, snow, snow, looking like play dough,
Snow, snow, snow, it looks like a white rainbow,
Snow, snow, snow, it is a white stereo.

Mohsin Imran (10)
Sneinton CE Primary School

Iceland Chills Approaching

Slippery slopes covered in snow
Does running through the flow
Up streams with a sparkling glow
What a wintry show!

Sheep skidding through the blow
Of a snowy storm loud as a stereo
Soft and slimy like bread dough
Prettier than a rainbow!

Wolves howling at the frost on their toes,
If Homer saw the cold, he'd say, 'Doh!
The storm's here, my only foe!
I think I should go back inside!'

Eilish Christine McSweeney (10)
Sneinton CE Primary School

Anger

Anger sounds like a stampeding rhino
Anger tastes like hot sauce
Anger smells like burning schools
Anger looks like a red raving rabbit
Anger is as big as an explosion.

Richie Clarke (9)
Sneinton CE Primary School

Anger

Anger sounds like a storm
Anger tastes like some blood
Anger smells like burning fire
Anger's colour is flaming red
Anger feels like a pokey bed
Anger reminds me of someone not listening to me
Anger is a liar, liar, liar
Never trust anger.

Nikoleta Rackova (9)
Sneinton CE Primary School

Love

Love is great and beautiful
It smells so sweet
When I see it, it looks so fantastic
It is sweeter than a cherry
My mum is dreaming of it every night
My mum is always phoning him up for a drink
And to go to the cinema
While my dad looks after me
How sweet is that!

Amber Wigman (8)
Sneinton CE Primary School

Anger

Anger is like a monster sleeping in my bed
Anger is like a devil sitting in my shed
Anger is a flame that doesn't take the blame
Anger is a ghost that hates you the most
But anger isn't friendly, anger's deadly
Anger creeps up behind
Anger will remind you of a scary thought.

Michaela Powis (9)
Sneinton CE Primary School

Horrible Hasty Hate

Hate is like a dark blue hairy tear
It tastes like stinky crabs
It smells like a rotten egg
It looks like a haunted house
It sounds like cymbals crashing together.

Yumi Li Vi (8) & Jasmine Wigman (7)
Sneinton CE Primary School

The Gleaming, Glowing Snow

Slippy, slimy silver snow,
Watch it glide and go and glow.

It froze my toe,
Like a piece of dough,
The snow is about,
The sloppy snow,
Wow, watch it flow,
It's going, going low.

Below the rainbow,
Glows the snow,
I'm holding the golden stereo,
Listening to my ridiculous foe.

The snowman brought me love and joy,
He's dead and it reminds me of the battle of Troy.

John Kazadi (10)
Sneinton CE Primary School

The Snow

When the snow blows,
It makes a glow.
All that snow,
Makes it a foe.
Slippery, sliding snow,
Is a foe.
The carnage,
The carnage of cars.
The fun,
Can be done.
The wonderful snow,
Is like a rainbow.
The people playing,
While it's snowing.

Gino Van Den Broecke (10)
Sneinton CE Primary School

Anger

Angry, angry Grandad, so angry
He's like a grumpy rhino
He moans and groans
He's got an angry wrath
That's an angry grandad
Angry creeps so quietly
It gets so quiet
It gets to you very quickly
It burns string in a snap
That's what.

Josh Taylor (9)
Sneinton CE Primary School

Love

Love feels like a dreaming of clouds
Love tastes like Heaven and peace
Love is faithful
Love looks like a pink heart
Love has a sweet smell
Love is beyond the world
Love is friendship and happiness
Love beats like the strong wind
Love reminds me of everything
Everything you need to know about love is here
What does love remind you of?

Sidra Ahmed (8)
Sneinton CE Primary School

I Feel Happy

It smells like fresh baked cookies
It tastes like fizzy sweet strawberries
It looks like blue sky
It sounds like a cheering crowd
It feels like a hug from a friend.

Isabelle Richardson (7)
Sneinton CE Primary School

Hate

Hate is like a stormy rain cloud
Hate looks like creepy rats
Hate sounds like thunder crashing
Hate tastes like monkey flies
Hate smells like dismal sewers.

Jack Sharp (7)
Sneinton CE Primary School

Hate

Hate is like a red-coloured tomato
It tastes like rotten eggs
It smells like gas
It looks like a fat, slimy snake.

Jasmine Hackett (7)
Sneinton CE Primary School

Fear Is A Horrible Feeling

Fear is dark red like blood
It tastes like mouldy chicken
It smells like a smelly bin
It looks like a spooky forest
It sounds like squelching footsteps
It feels like dry skin.

Owen Newton (8)
Sneinton CE Primary School

Slippy, Sloppy, Snow

Slippy snow
Falling in a row
The gleaming snow
Looks like a white rainbow
The snow is a tornado
Having fun
Slimy snow sliding
Sliding everywhere
The snow is an overgrown sheep
Snow is as heavy as ten boulders
Flowing in the snow.

Blake Campbell (10)
Sneinton CE Primary School

The Snowy Poem!

As I opened my window,
Snow dropped on my big toe,
The snow was as cold as ice,
It was like a winter wonderland,
As I excitedly walked out of my door,
I could feel my nerves tingling,
The snow was just like a show,
It saw the slippery snow slithering down the drain,
As I walked onto the snow,
I heard the wonderful crunching,
All my friends shouted, 'Yo!'
Whilst one said, 'Doh!'

Hayley Sylvia Cassady-Shillcock (10)
Sneinton CE Primary School

Beautiful Snow

The heavy snow started to settle softly,
A cat crunching its footsteps,
Marking its territory,
The snow is falling fiercely off trees and roofs,
The grass is asleep, the white blanket of snow covers it,
The snow is a tornado,
The monster of fun,
Now the fun has stopped,
The end . . .

Connor Storer-Fry (9)
Sneinton CE Primary School

The Snow

The snow is glass on the pavement
And on the road
My footprints make padded prints
On the floor
It flutters and flickers
As the snow meanders down
Falling silently to the ground.

Reece Clarke (10)
Sneinton CE Primary School

Falling Snow

Slimy
Slippery
Sloppy
Snow
Slimy
Slowly snowing
Silently
Falling to the
Ground
Everywhere
Is white.

Hannah Daisy Armitage (9)
Sneinton CE Primary School

Magical Snow

Snow, snow, snow
Is hard to blow
Falling softly on the ground
Slippy, slimy snow
Watching it glow.

Slippy, slimy, sliding, skiddy snow
Just watching the show
The crows go *whoa!*

Jo making angels
Mo shivering.

The snow bright as white play dough
Glowing in my eye.

On the trees are crows
Kicking off the snow on the branches
Below the tree is a girl with a bow
Hiding from her foes.

The snow is a tornado whizzing down from the sky
Sucking us up
Perhaps we might fly.

Bethany Steadman (10)
Sneinton CE Primary School

Love Poem

Love sounds like a cat sleeping
Love tastes like a lollipop
Love smells like some candy on a stick
Love looks like a rainbow in the sky
Love feels like you want to be nice to someone
Love is the colour pink
Love reminds me of being a baby
Love feels like there is a rainbow always shining over you
Love is like a light in my head
Love is the comfort of my bed
Love reminds me of when I am feeling happy.

Cavan Thomas (8)
Sneinton CE Primary School

Anger

Anger's like dirt
Anger's like a monster
Anger's like blood
Anger tastes like sick
Anger's like a lion
Anger's bad
Anger's horrible
Anger's like mud
Anger feels like you're getting hit
Anger's disgusting
Anger sounds like thunder and lightning
Anger smells like flames
Anger's like a tornado
Anger's like spikes
Anger reminds me of a storm
Anger is scary
Anger's slimy
Anger's like falling over.

Adam Davies (8)
Sneinton CE Primary School

Hate!

Hate is red like a big load of evil
It tastes like red blood
It smells like spider popcorn
It looks like a sloppy monster
It sounds like bombs dropping
It feels like wind blowing in my face.

Billie Rose (7)
Sneinton CE Primary School

Feeling Fear

Fear is horrible like green dirty grass
It smells like smelly socks
It looks dark like thunder
It sounds like thunder crashing
It feels like a bumpy spider.

Faizah Ahmed (8)
Sneinton CE Primary School

The Blackbird And Snow

As the snow sits simply still
The black-eyed bird shows no glow
For he's been covered in snow

After watching children play
He firmly flies away
Upon the rooftops he lays
Lovely lamp posts green and grey

Stalking carefully, crawling, crying
Wanting food like bread and brine
Pecking proudly on the window top
Chucking cheerfully, the woman gave her bread

When the snow went the black-eyed bird made her nest
And made her early eggs.

Shanice McKirgan (10)
Sneinton CE Primary School

Young Writers Information

We hope you have enjoyed reading this book - and that you will continue to enjoy it in the coming years.

If you like reading and writing poetry drop us a line, or give us a call, and we'll send you a free information pack.

Alternatively if you would like to order further copies of this book or any of our other titles, then please give us a call or log onto our website at www.youngwriters.co.uk

Young Writers Information
Remus House
Coltsfoot Drive
Peterborough
PE2 9JX

(01733) 890066